We've Go...

Sending Mail in the United States from Past to Present

Catherine Hinkson and Beth Beggs

Contents

Rigby
A Harcourt Achieve Imprint

www.Rigby.com
1-800-531-5015

When was the last time you wrote a note to a friend at school? Maybe you recently wrote a letter to a relative who lives in another state. Perhaps you sent an e-mail earlier today. You may have even sent a **text message** on your cell phone.

Today it is easy to communicate with someone many miles away. But in the early days of our country, sending a letter or a message to someone was much slower. Writing letters was the only way to send a message to someone far away.

Sending Letters in the Early United States

Imagine waiting weeks or even months to receive a letter. During **colonial** times that is what happened. There was no post office. People had to either deliver letters themselves or ask someone to do it for them. Travelers were often asked to take letters with them and drop them off in the towns they visited. Many times letters were dropped off in towns that were only *near* a letter's final **destination**. A letter could sit for weeks before another traveler picked it up and carried it where it needed to go.

If a letter needed to be sent a long distance, the sender had to find another way. The letter would often be left at a shop or an inn. From there, the letter might be taken on horseback, sent on a stagecoach, or sent up or down the river on a boat. Most roads were unpaved paths through the forest, so travel was both difficult and dangerous. As a result, sending a letter was slow and expensive.

Letters were often left at shops or inns to be taken to their destinations.

Actually getting a letter could be just as difficult as sending one. Letters were delivered to shops or inns, and the owner would hold the letter until someone came for it. That person might also have to pay for the letter.

Early letters did not have envelopes. The paper was folded and sealed with wax. The name and address were written on the outside of the letter.

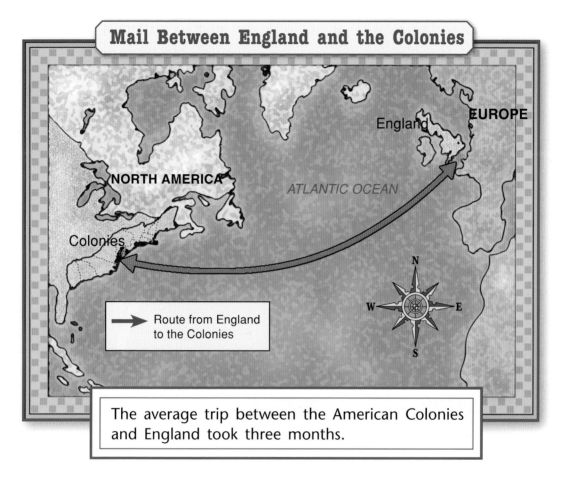

Mail Between England and the Colonies

EUROPE

England

NORTH AMERICA

ATLANTIC OCEAN

Colonies

→ Route from England to the Colonies

N
W — E
S

The average trip between the American Colonies and England took three months.

Some letters had to travel even farther. Many of the **colonists** still had friends and family in England to whom they wrote letters. These letters had to be sent on ships that were threatened by storms and pirates. If the letters made it to their destinations, the colonists would then have to wait for months to hear back. Imagine what it would feel like if you didn't hear from your family for months or even years.

In 1737 the British government named Benjamin Franklin the postmaster for the colonies. He built post offices throughout the colonies and improved the roads. These improvements sped up mail delivery. In addition, travelers were able to travel faster and more easily throughout the colonies because of these improved roads.

Benjamin Franklin was a newspaper publisher and scientist. He was postmaster under both the British and the United States governments.

By 1774, however, the colonists were becoming unhappy with the British postal system in the colonies. They wanted to start a new postal system that the colonies would run instead of the British government. William Goddard, a printer, set up another system for delivery of mail within the colonies. Soon, there were 30 post offices serving the colonies.

As the colonies became free from British rule, the founders of the new government knew that its citizens needed to be able to receive mail and information if they were to build a strong nation. So in 1775, the Continental Congress named Benjamin Franklin Postmaster General of the United States. The United States Postal Service that we know now also started on this day.

This post office in Philadelphia was the first post office in the American colonies.

In the first half of the 1800s, the people in the United States began moving to the new **territories** of Louisiana, Oregon, and California. Settlers in these areas wanted their mail and news to reach them just as fast as it had in the 13 original colonies. However, transportation across these territories was difficult because few trails were marked, and no railroads traveled to the West.

United States Territories, 1800

☐ Louisiana Territory
☐ Oregon Territory
☐ California
☐ Mexican Territory
☐ Northwest Territory
☐ Original 13 Colonies
☐ Florida Territory

To improve mail delivery to the western **settlements**, the government built new roads called post roads. In 1823 the government declared all waterways post roads, too. Steamboats and other boats that traveled the larger rivers such as the Mississippi helped deliver mail to areas with few roads.

Riverboats like this one delivered mail in the growing United States.

Riding with the Pony Express

When gold was found in California in 1848, a rush of people moved there to find their fortunes. Letters from the eastern states had to travel on ships around South America to reach the California settlers. Also, ships would sometimes take letters to Panama, send them over land to the Pacific Ocean, and then they would travel by ship to **ports** in California. From these ports, steamboats and messengers took the letters up the rivers to the smaller towns.

Gold was discovered in California in 1848. By the next year, people were rushing to the West to get rich. These people were called the Forty-Niners.

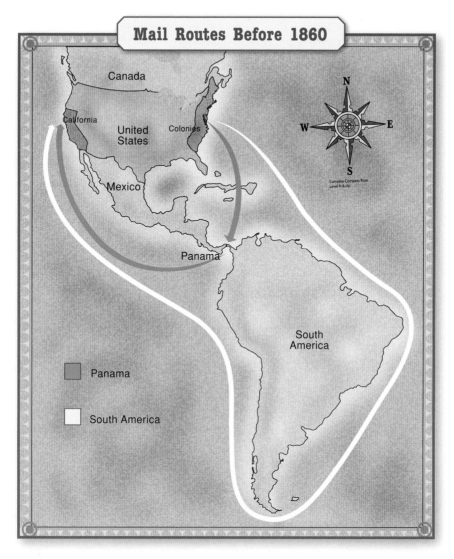

Mail Routes Before 1860

Canada

California

United States

Colonies

Mexico

Panama

South America

N
W — E
S

Complex Compass Rose
Level N & Up

Panama

South America

This process often took several months. The time could be made much shorter if the mail could be brought straight across the United States instead of around South America or through Panama. But how? One man thought he had the solution.

In 1860 William H. Russell came up with a plan to get the mail to the west coast more quickly. He hired boys who could ride horses very fast. These young men would carry the mail on horseback from Missouri to where the trail ended in California. Each rider would cover a part of the distance, handing the mail over to the next rider on the route.

PONY EXPRES

CHANGE OF
TIME!

NEWS!!

RED

RAT

10 Days to San Francisco!

LETTERS

WILL BE RECEIVED AT THE

OFFICE, 84 BROADWAY,

NEW YORK,

Up to 4 P. M. every TUESDAY,

AND

Up to 2½ P. M. every SATURDAY,

Which will be forwarded to connect with the PONY EXPRESS leaving
ST. JOSEPH, Missouri,

Every WEDNESDAY and SATURDAY at 11 P. M.

TELEGRAMS

Sent to Fort Kearney on the mornings of MONDAY and FRIDAY, will connect with PONY leaving St. Joseph, WEDNESDAYS and SATURDAYS.

EXPRESS CHARGES.

LETTERS weighing half ounce or under............$1 00
For every additional half ounce or fraction of an ounce 1 00
In all cases to be enclosed in 10 cent Government Stamped Envelopes,

And all Express CHARGES Pre-paid.

☞ PONY EXPRESS ENVELOPES For Sale at our Office.

New York, July 1, 1861.

WELLS, FARGO & CO., Ag'ts.

SLOTE & JANES, STATIONERS AND PRINTERS, 86 FULTON STREET, NEW YORK

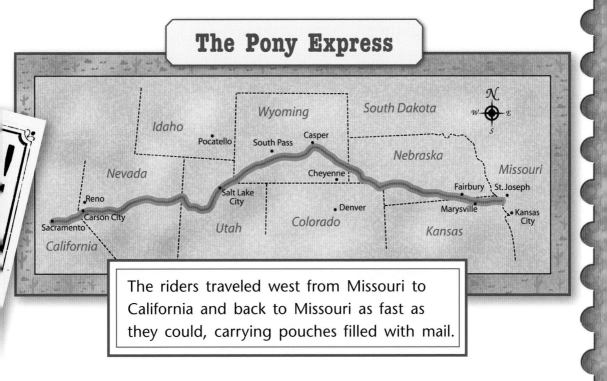

The Pony Express

The riders traveled west from Missouri to California and back to Missouri as fast as they could, carrying pouches filled with mail.

Not everyone thought Russell's idea would work, though. Most people thought traveling directly across the country was too dangerous. First there were no good maps of this area. Second the settlers were in conflict with many of the Native American groups who lived in the territory. Because of the conflict, people thought these groups might attack the young riders. However, Russell would not give into these doubts. He called his new company the Pony Express.

Because of the Pony Express, the mail was now practically flying across the prairies of the West! Riders would ride ten miles and then change horses at the next station. There were 165 stations along the route. Pony Express riders could ride ten miles in one hour and traveled 75 miles before handing the mail to another rider.

Pony Express riders had to weigh less than 125 pounds.

The Pony Express riders had special equipment to make their jobs easier. One piece of equipment was the mochila, which was a saddle cover that had with four pockets to hold mail. When a rider jumped onto a new horse, he would take his mochila with him.

The mochila was made from oiled silk to protect the letters. It was light and waterproof.

Sending a letter by horse sounds slow, but to the people of the 1800s, the Pony Express seemed like a miracle! It only took the Pony Express riders about ten days to make the same trip a stagecoach would make in twenty days. The fastest Pony Express trip happened in 1861. On this seven-day trip, riders delivered copies of the first speech given by the new president, Abraham Lincoln.

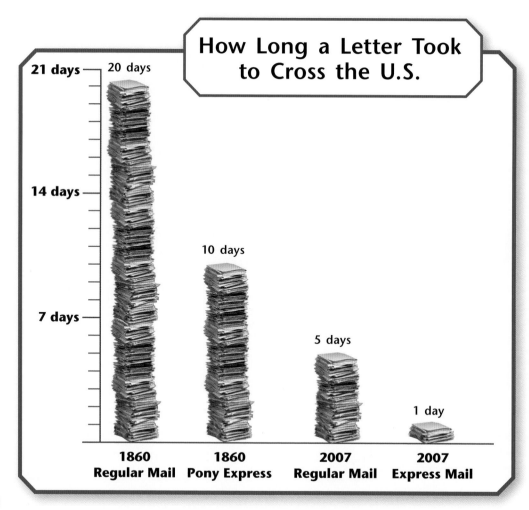

How Long a Letter Took to Cross the U.S.

1860 Regular Mail	1860 Pony Express	2007 Regular Mail	2007 Express Mail
20 days	10 days	5 days	1 day

In the same year Lincoln became president, a new technology threatened the Pony Express. The Pony Express was only a little more than a year old when this new invention put them out of business.

Abraham Lincoln came into office in 1861. People all over the United States waited for news about Lincoln's first speech.

Sending Messages by Telegraph

In 1861 Samuel Morse invented the **telegraph**. This machine used short and long electric signals to spell out words. These signals were called dots and dashes. These dots and dashes came to be called Morse Code.

Telegraph operators sent and received messages for other people. When a message came in, the operator would translate the dots and dashes into words, which they would then print on a **telegram**. The operators also sent messages by tapping out the letters on a telegraph key.

PACIFIC TELEGRAM

CLASS OF SERVICE

Full Rate   Day Letter   Night Letter

IF NEITHER OF THE TWO SYMBOLS SHOWN ABOVE APPEARS AFTER THE CHECK (NUMBER OF WORDS) THIS IS A FULL RATE
OTHERWISE ITS CHARACTER IS INDICATED BY THE SYMBOL APPEARING AFTER THE CHECK.

STOCKTON CALIF OCT 26 1948 79

TDPT 2 SAC VMA 10

MRS PHELPS WILKES.=

MERCY HOSPITAL SACRAMENTO CALIF.=

CONGRATULATIONS GALORE. WE ARE SO HAPPY FOR BOTH OF

TED ANNE AND TOMMY.=

800 AM.=

Messages sent by telegraph were printed out as telegrams.

Morse Code

A	.-	**N**	-.	**0**	-----
B	-...	**O**	---	**1**	.----
C	-.-.	**P**	.--.	**2**	..---
D	-..	**Q**	--.-	**3**	...--
E	.	**R**	.-.	**4**	....-
F	..-.	**S**	...	**5**	.....
G	--.	**T**	-	**6**	-....
H	....	**U**	..-	**7**	--...
I	..	**V**	...-	**8**	---..
J	.---	**W**	.--	**9**	----.
K	-.-	**X**	-..-		
L	.-..	**Y**	-.--		
M	--	**Z**	--..		

Key
- dash
• dot

When it was wartime in the United States, people wanted to hear news more quickly. Newspapers used the telegraph to send and receive stories about the war. Soon, people at home were using the telegraph to send messages to family members in other parts of the country. Before long, telegraph wires were strung all over the country!

Trains could carry passengers, mail, and goods faster than horses and coaches.

Although the telegraph delivered messages more quickly, people still sent most of their letters through the mail. Trains helped letters to travel even faster and to more locations than had horses and coaches.

At first Morse wanted to bury the telegraph wires. But after doing many experiments, he decided the best place for the wires was high in the air, strung between poles.

Mail on the Rail

In 1830 America's first steam train *Tom Thumb*, successfully carried more than 40 people, moving at about 10 miles an hour. The United States Post Office soon recognized the value of this new kind of transportation. By 1838 all railroads in the United States were used as mail routes.

Soon, every train carried mail in a special car.

Inside the mail car, the workers separated the mail into bags while the train moved to the next town.

At first only certain kinds of mail were sent on the railroad, and all of the sorting was done at post offices along the route. Gradually, this changed. The first "post offices on wheels," was put into use in 1864.

The train stopped at a station and the mail workers picked up the mail. They would then sort the mail in the mail car and put it into bags for **distribution** at the next station.

When a train didn't stop at a station, the worker on the train would kick the bag of mail off the train as it passed through. At the same time, another worker used a big hook to pick up any bags of mail waiting at that station.

By 1930 more than 10,000 trains were delivering mail in the United States. Every city, town, and village received mail this way, but people who lived in **rural** areas still found it difficult to send and receive mail.

Mail bags were often hung up on hooks so workers on the train could collect it while the train was moving through the station.

Rural Free Delivery allowed rural America to be connected to the cities.

It was hard to deliver mail to rural areas because there weren't many good roads. As a result, people often had to travel into town to pick up their mail. In 1893 the United States government decided to deliver the mail to homes outside of town. They called this program Rural Free Delivery, or RFD.

Not all areas were able to get RFD right away, however. Places where the roads were bad were still unable to get rural delivery. Between 1897 and 1908, many local governments spent millions of dollars repairing roads. In one county in Indiana, farmers themselves paid to improve a road in order to receive RFD.

Driving and Flying the Mail

Once RFD was underway, mail carriers in the rural areas had to provide their own transportation. They used horses and bicycles when the roads were good enough. By 1901 the post office was ready to start using the new "horseless wagons," or cars and trucks, for delivery.

The first mail delivery car took 35 minutes to go just over four miles. Even so, the post office was soon using "horseless wagons" to reach areas that could not be reached by train. Better roads and faster cars and trucks all made getting mail faster and easier.

The post office used cars such as this Model T to deliver mail to hard-to-reach areas of the United States.

In 1903 the Wright Brothers took their first airplane flight at Kitty Hawk, North Carolina. Fifteen years later, the United States government began to experiment with air delivery. The first air route delivered mail between New York and Washington, D.C.

In 1911 Earle Ovington became the first postal worker to use a plane to carry mail. He flew between Garden City and Mineola, New York, dropping mail bags from the plane for workers on the ground to pick up.

What's Next?

Today large post offices have equipment that helps workers do their jobs more quickly and easily. Special tubes and moving belts move heavy bags of letters and packages on and off of trucks. Machines read zip codes and use this information to sort the mail. These machines can even read handwriting!

Technology has made it much easier to sort large amounts of mail more quickly and with fewer mistakes.

Although technology has changed the way we communicate, Americans still use the postal system to send letters, magazines, and packages.

Will we someday be able to send packages through a computer? Who knows? Maybe you or someone you know will invent a technology that will make this possible!

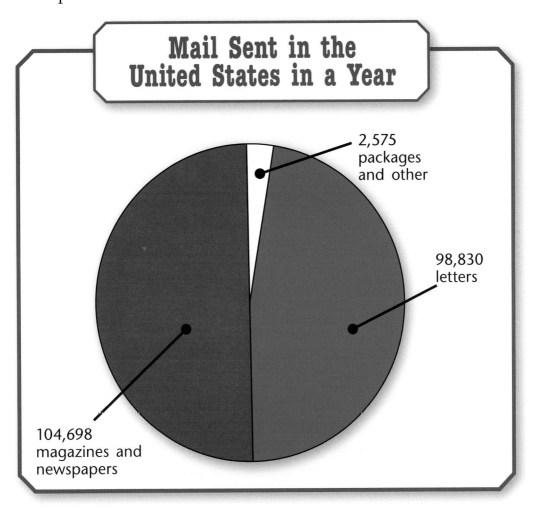

Mail Sent in the United States in a Year

2,575 packages and other

98,830 letters

104,698 magazines and newspapers

Glossary

colonial having to do with the time before America became its own country

colonists people who came from other countries to settle in America and form towns

destination the place where something is sent

distribution delivery

ports an area where ships load and unload things and people

rural the area outside a city or town

settlements farms and towns built bt people who have just moved into an area

telegram a message sent using a telegraph machine

telegraph a machine used to send message

territories areas of land that belonged to the United States but had not yet become states

text message a short message sent using a cell phone